Acts 20:24

SIN
ALWAYS
MATTERS

SIN
ALWAYS
MATTERS

The Cost of Sin and the Power of Grace

by Rick Burgess

published by

IRON HILL
press

Sin Always Matters: The Cost of Sin and the Power of Grace

©2024 by Rick Burgess. All rights reserved.

Published by Iron Hill Press in the United States of America.

Library of Congress Cataloging-in-Publication Data is on file at the Library of Congress, Washington, DC.

ISBN: 979-8-9857498-7-8

For all have sinned
and fall short
of the glory of God,
and are justified
by his grace as a gift,
through the redemption
that is in Christ Jesus.

ROMANS 3:23-24

CONTENTS

INTRODUCTION

I have the honor to be married to Sherri Burgess. She is a mighty woman of God who loves God's Word as much as anyone I have ever known. I am grateful for her impact on me, her husband, and her children. I am blessed to call her my wife, and my children are blessed to call her mom. The title of this devotional comes from a phrase that I've heard Sherri say to our children many times.

When she taught our children about making the right decisions, the importance of God's standard, and the blessing of His boundaries, she always said, "Listen to what I'm saying because sin always matters." This phrase stuck in my mind. "Sin always matters." Sin always matters to God. There's no circumstance where sin doesn't matter. There is no situation where God turns a blind eye toward sin. Sin matters, and it matters greatly. We have only to look at the cross should we ever doubt it.

The epicenter of God's plan to rescue Christians from sin is the day that Jesus, God's Son, was crucified. As a Christian, you've no doubt heard many references to the brutality of death by crucifixion. When we read the details of the various ways the Romans implemented crucifixion, we always recall horrific images of suffering and pain. Pondering this is never a comfortable experience.

In the case of Jesus, we know there were other shocking things He had to endure before He was even nailed to the tree. The crown of thorns. The whipping with the cat-o-nine-tails. Then the burden of the beam! How could He be asked to carry that bloody beam while so wholly exhausted from dehydration and blood loss? We know He was in bad shape because a man was asked to help bring that beam to the final place where they crucified Him.

I don't have the talent as a writer to accurately portray just how horrible a death Jesus chose to endure. But I want you to make sure you hear me say this: His physical death was not even the most painful part. Let me assure you that the most painful aspect of the cross was when our perfect, holy, righteous Savior took the sin of humankind of Himself and experienced the feeling of separation that sin causes between God and man. Jesus didn't cry out when He was scourged, beaten, or nailed to the cross. But when Jesus, fully God and fully man, felt the effects of sin, He exclaimed, "My God, my God, why have you forsaken me" (Matt. 27:46). Sin matters. Don't ever believe for one second that it doesn't.

However, don't miss an essential point from the previous paragraph. This truth is at the heart of our faith and this book. Notice I said that Jesus chose to endure the cross. Jesus willingly took on the cross, knowing what was coming His way. He did this, motivated by love for us, to fulfill the will of the Father, whose desire was to redeem humankind from the penalty of their sin. But for sinful humanity to return to a right relationship with God, provision must be made for sin.

You see, God is the holy life-giver. He is the creator of all things. We don't exist without Him. Not only is He the giver of all life, but He rules sovereignly over everything He creates. He didn't just bring us into being; He has ultimate authority over us. His rule is perfect. He isn't just a king; He is a perfectly righteous one. Every aspect of His character and His rule is 100% perfect. And if all this wasn't enough, God desired to create humankind and have humankind live in harmony with Him according to His ways. God's ways, His statutes, reflect His character. In other words, God's desire was and is for His created ones to live in such a way that their lives lined up with who He is.

What a powerful picture of God! We must remind ourselves of these truths because when we do, we understand exactly what sin is. Because God is the perfectly righteous, sovereign author of life who expects His creation to obey Him, sin isn't just a mistake. Sin isn't a goof-up. Sin isn't us just messing up. Sin is rebellion, plain and simple. And death is the only right and just consequence for rebellion against the sovereign, perfect Life-Giver. That's the only way to possibly balance the scales. This isn't because God is bloodthirsty or vindictive. It's not because He takes pleasure in punishing sinners (quite the opposite). No, death is the only proper consequence of sin because God is holy. There is no other result that is in balance with who God is.

All sin is rebellion against God, and all sin earns death. So, how is it that anyone is alive? Only by God's grace. God, in His grace, has made provision for the sins of humankind. For millennia, God, in His mercy, allowed His people to sacrifice an animal in their place. The sacrificial system was a powerful picture of grace. If I were a Jew living under the Old Covenant, I could take an animal to the Temple and sacrifice it, knowing that God saw the death of that animal as symbolic of my death. There is much grace in this. But God knew all along this system wasn't perfect. The writer of Hebrews points out that this sacrifice had to be made repeatedly and never provided true redemption or lasting justification. God knew this. He knew that the sacrificial system was a beautiful and painful foreshadowing of what was coming.

There came a day when God would make the ultimate provision for the sins of humankind, the day the perfect Lamb of God, Jesus, went to the cross to once and for all satisfy sin's dreadful requirement as the perfect sacrifice. And as we noted earlier, Jesus chose this. The Son obeyed the will of the Father, rescuing humankind from death. Jesus willingly chose to satisfy the requirements of the Law on our behalf to fulfill the will of the Father.

When you consider the misery of all that Jesus endured -- the agony of death and the pain of humankind's sin -- what is your reaction? Usually, our reaction to the brutality of the cross is something like, "Look how much God loves me!" This isn't a wrong reaction. The cross indeed demonstrates God's love, mercy, and grace. We can look to the cross and be very thankful for it. But the cross is also an event where we see God's response to sin. We see His perfect justice and wrath on display. And rather than shy away from it, we should look at it as boldly as we can, accepting it as just as much a part of God's character as His love and kindness. We will never understand the depth of God's love for us until we understand His absolute opposition to sin. Sin matters to God. It always matters.

Could I ask you for the next 31 days to read this devotional with the cross in mind, considering it a beautiful picture of God's grace and a stark reminder of how seriously God takes sin? The cross doesn't show us that God somehow lessened His view of sin or His need to perfectly address it. God didn't remove His wrath. He just poured it out on His Son so that those who believe in Him might be redeemed and reconciled to Him.

Sin always matters. When we fully grasp this, it changes how we see God and our lives.

PART 1

God, Sin, & Us

DAY 1
God's Attitude Toward Sin

> *[4] For you are not a God who delights in wickedness; evil may not dwell with you. [5] The boastful shall not stand before your eyes; you hate all evildoers. [6] You destroy those who speak lies; the LORD abhors the bloodthirsty and deceitful man.* - Psalm 5:4-6

How does God feel about sin? In a lot of ways, this is *the* question. We can't begin discussing our attitude toward sin without first dealing with God's attitude toward sin. In Psalm 5:4-6, David gives us a pretty clear view of God's opinion about sin, and it appears to blow the common phrase "God hates sin but loves the sinner" right out of the water. Does God extend His love to sinners? He does. If He didn't, none of us would be saved. But it is also true that God not only hates unrepentant sin but, according to His Word, hates the unrepentant sinner. How can this be true?

For starters, God hates sin because God is "holy, holy, holy" (Isa. 6:1-3, Rev. 4:8)! This doesn't mean God is somewhat holy. It means He is perfect, 100%, totally holy. And He cannot tolerate even the slightest hint of sin. He does not delight in wickedness.

1 John 3:9 says, "No one born of God makes a practice of sinning, for God's seed abides in him; and he cannot keep on sinning, because he has been born of God." Sometimes, we act like we've forgotten that when God redeems us through the debt Jesus Christ paid for us, God's seed now "abides" in us. For the Believer to live in unrepentant sin is to set yourself in opposition to God. God's hatred of wickedness should cause maximum conviction in our lives. How convicted of your sin are you?

What does this psalm say about those who continue to live in perpetual sin? It clearly says God "hated all evildoers." How do we reconcile this notion of God? Simple. God is perfect in all His attributes. God's love is perfect.

His mercy is perfect. His justice is perfect. And His hatred is perfect. God's hatred isn't like man's hatred. Even God's hatred toward sin is holy.

We live in a society that is so flippant about putting the individual first, mistreating others, lying about anything and everything, deceiving others just to get ahead or make a buck, and committing violence toward each other, devaluing human life as if we are playing a video game. These words from the Bible are saying something quite profound! This isn't just "bad behavior." This is sin. God hates all these things. I repeat: He hates it.

Does God allow sinful humankind to access His love and approval? Yes, He does. In His grace and mercy, He sent His Son, Jesus, to live a perfect life and die an atoning death so that through our faith in Him, we can be saved from the penalty of our sins. By repenting of our sin and placing our faith not in ourselves or our potential for goodness but in Jesus Christ, we can know God's endless and perfect love.

We have access to His grace, mercy, and love. And that truly is amazing. But does God love the defiant, perpetually rebellious, unrepentant sinner? According to His Word, He does not. Maybe today, the lesson for us is to commit to looking at the sin in our lives not as mistakes or slip-ups but as something that God truly hates.

DAY 2
What Is Sin?

> *[4] Yet I persistently sent to you all my servants the prophets, saying, 'Oh, do not do this abomination that I hate!' [5] But they did not listen or incline their ear, to turn from their evil and make no offerings to other gods.* - Jeremiah 44:4–5

We can't begin a book on our attitude toward sin without first considering what sin is. God's relationship with the Old Testament prophet Jeremiah is a compelling example of this.

God was constantly telling Jeremiah to deliver bad news to His people. God's people had largely abandoned Him. God was calling them back to Himself and promising judgment if they did not stop following other gods. The people hated Jeremiah and his messages as a result. But the worst thing the people did was to ignore God's warnings. In doing so, they brought the wrath of God on themselves. In their actions, we see the same problem humankind has been dealing with since the Fall in the Garden of Eden.

God told Adam and Eve exactly how to live. He provided everything they needed to live in peace and harmony with each other and with God. But there was one thing God did not give them. They did not have the authority to choose right from wrong. They were to trust that the God that created them would dictate what was right and wrong, what was good and what was evil.

Don't lose sight of the fact that this was God looking after them. God wasn't trying to be a killjoy. God's barriers are blessings. Too often, we see God's barriers as something keeping us from pleasure when, in reality, they are keeping us from destruction. Adam and Eve, and all who have followed, decided they wanted to have a say on what was right and wrong. Remember that God's standard is always correct, but that wasn't good enough for Adam and Eve and is not good enough for people today.

God told His people through the prophet Jeremiah not to go to Egypt and to discontinue the worship of idols, or God would bring not His love and protection but His anger and wrath. He clearly laid out the path back to a proper relationship with Him that would lead to their good. Yet, they rejected His instructions. They made it clear that they enjoyed these pagan practices and that they would continue the practice.

Of course, this is a sin. Ignoring God's instructions is a sin. Doing that which God says not to do is a sin. Not doing what God says to do is sin. And as human beings, we are really, really good at this. We don't think being under God's perfect, benevolent authority is best for us. Like Adam and Eve in the garden, we reject God's instructions and desire to follow our ways. We see this lived out in countless different ways every day.

For example, God clearly says that for a man's own good, he should be sexually pure and that sexual intimacy should be something that is reserved for his wife. This is not because God is trying to withhold pleasure from us. He is instead trying to protect us. He makes it clear that if we follow His standard, it will produce physical pleasure and beautiful, pure intimacy with the woman He has ordained for us to be with. But far too many times, men say, "No, thank you, God Almighty. I am wiser than you. I will pursue this pleasure whenever and with whomever I choose." What is the result? Regret, broken relationships, children born outside of marriage, and so on. Sexual intimacy is just one area where man consistently disregards God's instructions. We could go on and on.

Here's a tip for you: God's ways are always right. When He sets boundaries, these boundaries are blessings. He is perfect, and we are flawed. When we reject His instructions, we are ultimately rejecting Him. Failing to follow His ways, i.e., sinning, is always wrong. There are consequences for our sins, sometimes grave consequences. There were for God's people when they ignored Jeremiah's warnings. Sin always matters.

DAY 3
God's Response to Sin, Part 1

> *And the LORD regretted that he had made man on the earth, and it grieved him to his heart.* - Genesis 6:6

I remember the conversation well. I was talking to a man who was recommending a podcast to me. The more he shared, the more I recognized that the teaching communicated on this podcast was Christian universalism. Sadly enough, this has become far too popular in many circles. To simplify it, Christian universalism is the theological position that God loves human beings so much that He has forgiven all of us, and everyone, regardless of their behavior or religious beliefs, is going to heaven. Christian universalism says that there should not be a concern that any human is going to hell. After all, how could a loving God do anything that would negatively affect people?

The man hadn't gotten far in the podcast yet, but the bait was on the hook. He reminded me that we shouldn't forget that God has always loved us and that the most important thing to remember is that God would never do anything to us that wasn't loving. Imagine his surprise when I asked, "Then what do you make of that time that God killed everyone on the earth but eight people"?

Let me be obvious: I wasn't trying to insinuate that God wasn't loving. He is perfectly loving and incapable of doing anything that contradicts this aspect of His nature. But God is also perfectly just. And because this is so, He must respond to sin perfectly.

What we read in Genesis 6, the story that I was recounting to the man in my example, is God's response to sin. And what we see is His perfect wrath on display. The sin of humanity had become so repulsive to our Holy Creator that He regretted making us. God so hated the wickedness of humankind that He exercised His wrath and sent a flood to kill all but the most righteous, i.e., Noah and his family. This is an example of God's wrath.

There is another moment in Scripture where we see God's perfect response to sin. Later, in the Gospels, we discover God sending His only Son, Jesus, to receive the Father's wrath so that those who believe in Him might be spared from eternal punishment and be made fully righteous in His eyes. These two responses are both perfectly in line with who God is.

So, is God loving and merciful toward sinful humanity? Yes. Perfectly so. Does God respond in wrath toward sin? Yes. Both can be true! For some reason, human beings have decided that God's love and mercy are somehow more easily tolerated than God's wrath and judgment. And yet, only a proper understanding of God's wrath and judgment can make our understanding of His grace, mercy, and love so powerful!

Do we see God's mercy in Genesis 6:1-8? We do. Genesis 6:8 tells us that Noah found favor in the eyes of the Lord. God told Noah to build an ark because a flood was coming to destroy the earth and all who rejected God. Noah and his family were to get on the ark so that they would be saved when God's wrath came in the form of a flood. God said He would establish a covenant with Noah because he deemed Noah righteous. Why? The answer is in Genesis 7:5: "And Noah did all that the LORD had commanded him." Was Noah righteous because he believed God wanted him to build the ark and gather the animals? Yes. But his belief motivated his actions. He was deemed righteous because he did what God said. His belief, his faith, saved him.

But what about those people who were consumed by God's wrath? Why was God not merciful to them? Let me remind you that God had Noah build the ark over decades. During those years, people mocked Noah, and they did not heed God's warning to get on the ark in order to also be saved. God extended mercy, but humankind rejected it. As a result, their choice led them to experience God's wrath.

What about us? Don't be mistaken: everyone who does evil in God's sight and rejects the redemption provided by the ultimate ark, Jesus, will one day experience God's perfect wrath. And yet, in His great mercy, God stands willing to extend saving grace to any sinner who repents and submits in faith to Christ. This is who God is and how He responds to sin.

DAY 4
God's Response to Sin, Part 2

[7] The one who conquers will have this heritage, and I will be his God and he will be my son. [8] But as for the cowardly, the faithless, the detestable, as for murderers, the sexually immoral, sorcerers, idolaters, and all liars, their portion will be in the lake that burns with fire and sulfur, which is the second death. - Revelation 21:7–8

Revelation 21:7-8 is near the end of John receiving the revelation from the Lord. John has just seen the new heaven and earth, and Jesus has told him that He is making everything new. One of the ways Jesus will make all things new is to remove all who have rebelled against Him: Satan, the antichrist, the false prophet, demons, and every single human being who refused to repent and chose their sin over the redemption provided by Jesus. Due to their refusal to repent, their sin will condemn them to eternal separation from God.

In verses 7-8, God describes the types of people who will spend eternity separated from Him. When we look at the list, do you notice which sin is listed first? The cowardly. My wife Sherri pointed this out to me one day, and I had never noticed it when I read Revelation 21. Who are the cowardly? Those who lack the boldness to stand against the world and stand in faith with Christ. They crumble to the standards of the world and the demands of their flesh. Instead of denying themselves, picking up their cross, and entering the narrow gate to follow Jesus, they view the desires of the flesh and the applause of the world as more important than being right with God. Maybe they didn't think God was real. Perhaps they thought He was and that He'd forgive them anyway because He loves them just like they are. Whatever the case, what God tells John in these verses is that the cowardice of the unbeliever will doom them to hell.

In yesterday's devotional, we learned that one way God responds to sin is His wrath. Today, we see that another of God's responses to sin is to condemn the sinner to eternal separation from Him. This is, of course, known as hell. God doesn't condemn the unrepentant sinner to hell because He wants to torture them or make them pay for their sin in some form of retribution. Nowhere in the Bible does it say God takes joy in condemning sinners to hell. God condemns sinners to eternal separation from Him because, in His absolute holiness, He cannot be in relationship with anything that isn't also holy. In His grace, He has made the Gospel known so that anyone who submits in faith to His Son, Jesus, can be saved and restored to perfect fellowship with Him. But there are consequences for sin. Apart from faith in Christ, we cannot be in union with God.

People will say, "God meets us right where we are." This is, of course, true. But so often, that phrase is used to excuse our sin. Here's a more accurate statement: God meets us right where we are, but He does not leave us there. He delivers us from our sins. The cowardly can know God. They can be transformed by faith and be welcomed into a relationship with Him. But many times, the cowardly won't be redeemed because they simply love sin so much that they will never give it up, not even to be in the presence of God. The list continues with those who have no faith in God, wicked people who do evil, detestable things, murderers, the sexually immoral, those who tamper with witchcraft, those who love, value, serve, or fear something more than God, and those who lie and never change. They loved their sin more than God, and it cost them their eternity.

For some people, sin will never matter on this side of eternity. Ultimately, their unrepentant sin will earn God's wrath and eternal separation from Him. Is it fun to ponder these truths? Is it uplifting? Is it encouraging? No. It isn't. But to understand God's love, mercy, and grace, we must understand His response to sin.

DAY 5
The Need for a Provision

[17] For God did not send his Son into the world to condemn the world, but in order that the world might be saved through him. [18] Whoever believes in him is not condemned, but whoever does not believe is condemned already, because he has not believed in the name of the only Son of God. - John 3:17–18

John 3:16 is one of the most well-known verses in Scripture, and rightly so because it is really good news. But John 3:17-18 is also a vital part of the Gospel message. We will continue to talk about the many reasons that sin always matters. But here, we must grasp what may be the most important reason: sin matters because unless Jesus redeems us, we are condemned by our sin. Do not miss this: we cannot rectify our sin problem outside God's provision of Jesus. Our best efforts will only ever fall miserably short.

In this passage, Jesus clarifies why His Father sent Him into the world. Without the debt Jesus paid for humankind, we are condemned. We need a Savior! Why? Because we need to be saved! From what? Sin! God is holy. We are not. And because we will never be holy, we will always be incapable of saving ourselves. Always. The solution to our sin problem has to come from outside of us.

God's plan was always for Jesus to solve humankind's sin problem. Jesus clearly says that if we genuinely believe in Him, we can escape sin's condemnation. Two days ago, we read about God pouring out His holy wrath on sin. One of the most powerful truths of the Gospel, one we'll get into deeper tomorrow, is that God chose to pour out His wrath on His sinless Son, Jesus, for the sake of all who believe in Him. For those who believe in Jesus, the wrath He took from God was taken on their behalf (Rom. 5:9). This is amazing grace!

When these verses say people need to "believe" in Jesus, this doesn't simply mean they believe He historically existed. People can't only believe Jesus was a good guy and a good teacher. For the atoning sacrifice Jesus made on humankind's behalf to be credited to someone, they must believe that Jesus was the Son of God, no less than God Himself. The belief in Jesus that redeems us is a belief that includes trusting and obeying. We turn from sin, leave faith in our authority, and fully commit to God's authority. We submit to His authority and believe that only He can redeem us. We acknowledge we cannot redeem ourselves. We believe that Jesus paid the debt that our sin owed, and only by the grace of God provided in Him can we be saved from the condemnation we deserve. Did you get that? We don't deserve to be redeemed, but by the grace of God through our faith in Jesus, we can be redeemed. That's what Jesus meant when He said He wasn't sent to condemn the world. He didn't have to; we were already condemned due to sin.

Jesus Christ, the Messiah, came to save humankind from the results our sin rightfully earned us. Sin matters so much that Jesus died for it. He is the only solution for our sin problem. Without Jesus, we are hopelessly and eternally lost in our sin.

DAY 6
God's Perfect Provision

Since, therefore, we have now been justified by his blood, much more shall we be saved by him from the wrath of God. - Romans 5:9

Yesterday, we focused on the idea that Jesus was God's "plan A" to redeem humankind from our sins. We learned that we cannot do anything about our sin problem on our own. Every human being is born with a sin-nature. This is our spiritual inheritance from Adam. Because we are all sinners, we rightfully deserve God's judgment. We've covered this pretty well to this point. God is holy. He cannot ever cease to be holy. Even the "smallest" sin makes us unholy. Not only can the unholy not be in fellowship with God, they cannot even enter the presence of God. And if God left it at that, we'd be hopeless and helpless. Praise God that He didn't leave it at that.

Men, we must not take sin lightly. Take a moment and read Romans 5:8-10. Here, we see another look at exactly what Jesus saved us from. Paul is essentially celebrating the fact that through Jesus, God resolved the hopeless situation our sin put us in. Let's pause and closely examine how miraculous God's solution was.

We've established that sin is such a big deal that it earns God's wrath on every human being. But God was not content with leaving us there. Because of His great love for us, God Himself took on human flesh, becoming 100% human while remaining 100% God, to become the very sacrifice demanded by His holiness! Just sit in the truth that God poured the wrath you and I deserved onto His own Son for a moment. We cannot misunderstand this crucial point. God didn't change His mind or dilute His holiness in order to make things right between Him and us. He did not withhold His wrath. He poured it out on the Son, who perfectly satisfied the Father's sense of justice due to the sinless life He lived on this earth. Jesus took the sin of the world on Himself, allowing God's judgment to be fulfilled.

Now, let's get deep. We know that God is triune. We know He exists in three distinct persons, the Father, the Son, and the Holy Spirit, but without any separation. This truth means God poured out the judgment due to you and me on Himself. What grace! What mercy! What love!

But if that weren't enough, don't miss what Paul says in verse 8. God didn't wait for us to clean ourselves up and come to Him. He extends this amazing, wonderful, unbelievable grace to us while we are still dead in our sins. Despite our sin, God wipes our debt clean; this is what Paul means when he says we've been justified. God applied the wrath reserved for us on Jesus and imparted to us Jesus' righteousness. By doing so, God reconciled us to Himself. In other words, our relationship with Him is restored through faith in Christ.

If I'm honest, God's grace and mercy are much harder for me to understand than His wrath. His wrath makes perfect sense to me. We rebelled against a holy God. We deserve punishment. No, I find the grace and mercy hard to comprehend. It is almost beyond my ability to grasp. Knowing what God has done for you and me, how could we ever be apathetic about the idea of redemption? How could we ever be anything other than on fire to love, worship, and serve God fully?

DAY 7
Accessing God's Provision

> *[15] We ourselves are Jews by birth and not Gentile sinners; [16] yet we know that a person is not justified by works of the law but through faith in Jesus Christ, so we also have believed in Christ Jesus, in order to be justified by faith in Christ and not by works of the law, because by works of the law no one will be justified.* - Galatians 2:15–16

We've made a good case up to this point for what sin is, how God responds to sin, and how God provides a solution for our sin problem. In today's devotional, I want to discuss how we access God's provision, namely, a saving relationship with Jesus.

Most men are wired to be problem solvers. This works to our benefit in a lot of situations. But when it comes to our faith, it can work against us. As men, we love to look at a problem, develop a strategy, and map out the steps to solve the problem or accomplish the goal. We picture the outcome we want, believing we can achieve it if we give our all and lay everything on the line. This may work great for accomplishing earthly goals. But it's a recipe for disaster in our spiritual lives. When it comes to solving our sin problem, we can do nothing on our own. Even our best efforts to justify ourselves through keeping rules and regulations will always fall terribly short.

Faith in ourselves is a mistake we all make far too many times. When we place our faith in our ability to follow moral rules, we play a dangerous game. We will only wind up frustrated and hopeless, thinking we can do what only God can do. Paul reminds us in these Galatian verses that justification will never come from faith in our behavior and strength. Only by putting our faith in Jesus can we be saved from the penalty of our sins.

Scripture destroys any notion that we could ever be so wonderful that we might earn our redemption. Paul points us to the only solution for our salvation: faith in Jesus Christ. Jesus Christ did what we will never be able to do. He lived a perfect life, satisfying God's requirements. In His grace, God allows Jesus' righteousness to be counted for us if we only believe in Him. We can never earn our salvation. Only by faith in Jesus are we saved. Jesus alone has the power to transform all who place their faith in Him.

If this sounds simple, it is. That's the beauty of the Gospel. But don't be fooled by the kind of faith Jesus demands. It's a faith of action. To truly place our faith in Jesus, we must turn from our sin and repent, deny ourselves, submit to His Lordship, and leave our authority. This is what true faith in Jesus looks like. It's not a passive faith. It's a faith that compels action.

Jesus says we must count the cost before we place our faith and trust in His authority. What could our faith cost us? Friends, family, a job, comfort, and so on. For some people, this can be a burden. They struggle to honestly believe that submission to Christ will be better than some of those sins they love more than Him. This is where faith comes in. Do you have enough faith to leave your authority and abilities and genuinely believe that Jesus is enough? Jesus justifies us, not our works. Jesus and Jesus alone.

Do you believe in Jesus, or are you still placing your faith in yourself? If you are still placing your faith in yourself, can I ask you a question? How is that going? Accept God's grace, and drop the ill-fated plans you have to somehow earn God's favor. Place your faith in Jesus, and He will justify and transform you into a new creation. Will it cost you? Yes. It will. But what you gain far outweighs anything you will lose in the process.

DAY 8

Sin Requires Repentance

> *[2] And he answered them, "Do you think that these Galileans were worse sinners than all the other Galileans, because they suffered in this way? [3] No, I tell you; but unless you repent, you will all likewise perish.* - Luke 13:2–3

In Luke 13:3, Jesus makes a powerful statement about why sin matters. Jesus is being asked about an incident that has generated a lot of scholarly debate over the centuries. What scholars can agree on is that at some point, Pilate, the Roman governor of Judea at the time of Christ, murdered a group of Galileans as they were making sacrifices in the Temple. How and why this happened has for centuries been a source of debate. The issue is that people during this time believed that tragedy, especially this kind of horrific event, was God's judgment on people's sins. Jesus is speaking out against this idea.

Jesus' response in verse 2 is to ask a rhetorical question: "Do you think these folks were being punished because they were greater sinners than anyone else? Absolutely not." Then Jesus says something powerful to the crowd. He basically says that the thing they need to worry about is their sin. Jesus sets them straight by making one thing very clear: sin condemns, and everyone must repent of their sin in order to be redeemed. Jesus points out that all of us, regardless of our earthly status, are in equal need of redemption. Therefore, all must repent or perish.

Sin matters. If we want eternal life and not death, repentance is necessary. This is important to understand because the preaching of repentance seems to be fading in our modern culture. Paul warned us about this in his second letter to Timothy. In 2 Timothy 4, Paul warns Timothy that the day will come when people will no longer endure sound teaching and will instead seek out teachers to suit their passions. If a pastor is motivated by attendance, preaching repentance might be an obstacle. And yet, Jesus Himself preached repentance to all He encountered.

In Acts chapter 2, we find the beginning of the Church after the Holy Spirit has been poured out. Peter is preaching with a power he never had before. When Peter finishes the message, Scripture tells us that the people's hearts were cut (vs. 37), meaning they were convicted of their sins by the Holy Spirit. Conviction comes from the Holy Spirit; shame comes from the adversary. Conviction leads to repentance, which leads to redemption. Too often, shame leads to a false sense that we cannot be forgiven; the accuser uses the sins of our past to render us hopeless and unable to impact our faith. We are all equal at the foot of the cross, in equal need of redemption. Yes, we must repent, but if we are willing to turn from our sins and put our faith in the Lordship of Jesus Christ, He will forgive us.

Paul puts it best in Romans 8:1: "There is therefore now no condemnation for those who are in Christ!" So, if we repent in faith (and we must), our past sins are forgiven, and the power of that sin to condemn us has been removed by the sacrifice provided by Jesus Christ. Praise His holy name! Yes, sin always matters, but thanks to Jesus, sin can also be forgiven.

PART 2

The Results of Sin

DAY 9
Freed From Sin, Not to Sin

[7] For one who has died has been set free from sin . . . [11] So you also must consider yourselves dead to sin and alive to God in Christ Jesus. [12] Let not sin therefore reign in your mortal body, to make you obey its passions. - Romans 6:7, 11–12

In Romans 6:7, 11-12, Paul is clarifying something that seems to be an ongoing problem with us. Simply put, we don't understand the power of God's grace. In Romans 6:1-2, Paul is furious that some of those who had been saved by faith in Christ adopted some flawed theology that suggested they had been given a pass to continue in sin. This was a struggle with Paul's original audience. And it is a struggle with us.

It is true that even those of us whom Christ has redeemed still struggle with our sin-nature, and we will until we join God in eternity. But Paul is warning us that we have been given power over the sin in our lives due to new life in Christ. He says that the sinner in Christ has been set free from the bondage of sin, not just in the eyes of God, but in how we see ourselves. Paul says we should consider ourselves dead to sin and alive to God in Christ Jesus. He goes on to say in verse 12 that we are not to let sin reign in our mortal bodies. He says don't let your body make you obey its flawed passions.

When we go on perpetually and deliberately sinning, giving in to our flesh, we are taking the grace that Jesus went to the cross to provide for us and abusing that grace. We are saying to Jesus, "Hey, thank you for taking the Father's perfect wrath that I deserve. But the ugly sin you bore for me? I am still doing it." The saddest part of all this is what we say to the Spirit. When we continue to habitually commit the same sin repeatedly, we're telling the Holy Spirit that we're not interested in living out the new life He's working to provide us.

How can we take sin so lightly and consider grace to be so cheap? The fight against sin in our lives isn't something we do to earn our salvation. No, that's impossible. The fight against sin in our lives is a result of our salvation. Our salvation, justification, reconciliation, and redemption all give us access to the power of God, who removes sin from our lives. He changes our desires. So, if this isn't happening, you may just refuse to embrace this new life.

Are you feeding the sins that put Jesus on the cross? Or are you starving them? Sin matters. So instead of feeding your flesh, feed the new spirit you have been given by faith in Christ Jesus.

DAY 10

Sin Leads to Destruction

> *But when he was strong, he grew proud, to his destruction. For he was unfaithful to the LORD his God and entered the temple of the LORD to burn incense on the altar of incense.* - 2 Chronicles 26:16

Uzziah became king of Judah (the southern kingdom) when he was only 16. We read in 2 Chronicles 26 that the Lord was pleased with him as king and blessed him with incredible success against the enemies of Judah because he was one of the very few kings who did what was right in the eyes of the Lord. But unfortunately, like many people God decides to bless, Uzziah went from "How great is God?" to the very dangerous "How great am I."

Due to God giving him so much victory and success, Scripture tells us Uzziah's fame spread far and wide. But then look at 2 Chronicles 26:16. Uzziah's God-given strength led to his pride and destruction. In the second half of 2 Chronicles 26:16, we see that Uzziah did something he never should have done. He was unfaithful to the Lord and would now do something he knew he was not supposed to do. We might benefit from a little background context: the sons of Aaron were ordained by God to be the priests in His tabernacle and later in the Temple. They alone had been consecrated to burn incense at the altar of incense, which signified the prayers of the people being offered to God. It didn't matter that Uzziah was king. This was not his role. It was forbidden for anyone other than the priests to make this offering.

Uzziah was so full of himself, foolishly thinking that his fame and accomplishments were a credit to his ability and not God's favor, that he decided to do whatever he wanted, including now burning the incense at the altar. Azariah, the priest, tried to stop Uzziah, going as far as to bring 80 other priests to try to stop him from sinning against God. These priests warned the king to turn around and leave the sanctuary so he wouldn't dishonor God. Did Uzziah listen and thank the men for loving him enough to turn him away from the destruction of sin? No, he got angry. Uzziah pushed through the priests with the censer in hand to burn the incense. What happened? The Lord struck him with leprosy, and due to his arrogance and disobedience, he was a leper living in seclusion, excluded from the house of the Lord until his death. The very same people who once admired and even envied Uzziah were now repulsed by him. He wanted to be remembered not for his devotion to God but for his fame and fortune. But due to his sin, he was only remembered as the guy whom God struck with leprosy.

Proverbs 16:18 is usually quoted out of order. People typically say that pride comes before a fall, but that's not what the verse says. The verse says pride comes before destruction and a haughty spirit before a fall. Uzziah's pride led to his destruction. Now, God is merciful to us modern-day Uzziahs by placing people in our lives who attempt to hold us accountable. Do you have those people? I surely do, and I am grateful for them. But to benefit from those people, we have to listen to them. Uzziah had Azariah. But Uzziah ignored him.

Have you ever disregarded those people God placed in your life to keep you from sinning against Him? Brothers, these people are gifts from God! While it's not easy, accepting the rebuke of a brother can save you so much trouble and keep you on a path honorable to God.

Have you ever tried to help someone who disregarded your instruction from the Lord? Proverbs 9:8 calls these people scoffers. "Do not reprove a scoffer, or he will hate you; reprove a wise man, and he will love you." Which one are we? Scoffers attack or mock anyone who tries to hold them accountable. We can't be a scoffer, but we also can't give up on scoffers. Sin matters too much for either of those things to be a reality.

Let us never forget that the unchecked sin of pride always leads to our destruction.

DAY 11
Sin Makes Us Enemies of God

> *[5] I myself will fight against you with outstretched hand and strong arm, in anger and in fury and in great wrath* . . . *[8] "And to this people you shall say: 'Thus says the LORD: Behold, I set before you the way of life and the way of death. [9] He who stays in this city shall die by the sword, by famine, and by pestilence, but he who goes out and surrenders to the Chaldeans who are besieging you shall live and shall have his life as a prize of war.*" - Jeremiah 21:5, 8-9

God has always loved His people enough to discipline them. Why do we read so often about Him disciplining His people? Because of their defiant sin. Jeremiah warned the people that God was fully aware of their sin, which angered Him. Like any scoffer, the reaction to this warning wasn't a "thank you for informing me of God's anger at my obvious sin." It was to attack the messenger. That is the problem with scoffers; they are so prideful that they are unwilling to see the truthfulness of the message. The correct response, of course, would have been brokenness that led to repentance.

Jeremiah records another occasion where God's people have chosen sin over loyalty to Him, and God brings His wrath upon their defiance. It's how God chose to do this that is so stunning. God chose to discipline His people by using one of their enemies. Don't miss that point, brothers. God makes it clear that though the Chaldeans will do the damage, they are being used as the strong arm of God. If that doesn't attest to God's sovereign will, I don't know what does.

When our sin against others is noted, it's often rightfully pointed out as bad behavior. But what is missing is who we truly sin against. You see, most of the time, we justify our sin by refusing to acknowledge that we are actually sinning against God. Jeremiah's message to God's people concerning their sins is the same for us today: "I set before you the way of life and the way of death. Which way do you choose?"

The Bible clearly states that sin earns death (Rom. 6:23). God said, through Jeremiah, that if His people refused to surrender to the wrath that He was bringing, they would die. He said that they must leave the city and submit to being prisoners so that, though they would be a prize of war, they would live. God would deal with the Chaldeans for their wickedness later. But His primary concern was the repentance of His people.

God loved His people so much that He was willing to use their enemies to wake them up. We would be deeply mistaken if we don't think God works the same way today. Yes, if we have been saved by faith in Christ, we have been saved from God's judgment. Jesus took the judgment our sin earned upon Himself. We never have to fear that our sin will earn us death. Paul says in Romans 8 that for those in Christ, there is nothing in all creation that can separate us from the love of God (Rom. 8:31-39). That includes our sin. We don't have to fear death. But we should have a reverent fear over God's discipline. God loves us immensely. And God, like any good father, disciplines those He loves.

One of the most instructive ways God chooses to discipline us is that He often relents from saving us from the consequences of our sins. Sin always makes a mess, and God will often allow us to experience the consequences of our sins to steer us toward repentance. As God's children, those whom Jesus has redeemed, we can never be angry or frustrated at God for allowing us to experience the consequences of our sins. Instead, we have to approach God with a willingness to acknowledge our sin, especially recognizing that any sin is a sin against God.

Brother, we must never let the consequences of our sin cause us to turn against God. God has allowed me to experience the consequences of my sin, and I can tell you that I have never been angry with God as a result. I have, however, been angry with myself for being so sinful that I put God in a position where He had to allow consequences in order to turn me to repentance.

DAY 12
Sin Produces Earthly Consequences

[9] Why have you despised the word of the LORD, to do what is evil in his sight? You have struck down Uriah the Hittite with the sword and have taken his wife to be your wife and have killed him with the sword of the Ammonites. [10] Now therefore the sword shall never depart from your house, because you have despised me and have taken the wife of Uriah the Hittite to be your wife. - 2 Samuel 12:9–10

By now, we have firmly established that God hates sin. So, here's a question for you and me: If it's true that God hates sin, then why do we take it so lightly? The worst example is when you see someone playing the "David Card." What's the David Card? It's when someone God has entrusted with a leadership position commits a sin and immediately wants to be put right back in their role of influence for the church or a ministry.

David committed some horrible sins. And it wasn't just limited to the events surrounding Bathsheba, though we'll focus our attention there for this devotional. The guys who want to pull the David Card like to point out that David grievously sinned when it came to Bathsheba. And yet, God forgave him and still used him. Of course, this is all true. But these men seem to conveniently ignore the earthly consequences of David's sin.

People who pull the David Card love 2 Samuel 12:13: "David said to Nathan, 'I have sinned against the LORD.' And Nathan said to David, 'The LORD also has put away your sin; you shall not die.'" They love it and shout it at anyone who tries to make them own up to the consequences of their sin. But they never seem willing to quote from verses 9-12. And boy, do they flee from verses 14-15: "[14] Nevertheless, because by this deed you have utterly scorned the LORD, the child who is born to you shall die." [15] Then Nathan went to his house. And the LORD afflicted the child that Uriah's wife bore to David, and he became sick." Notice that God hasn't addressed Bathsheba as David's wife yet. God calls her Uriah's wife as he hands out the earthly consequences of David's sin. Not only is David informed of the consequences of His sin, but God also reminds David why this is happening. Our sin produces earthly consequences.

Does Bathsheba become David's wife? Yes, she does. Does she give birth to Solomon? Yes, she does. Is David forgiven for his sins? Blessedly, He is. But none of this changes the fact that long-lasting earthly consequences would plague David's life for the rest of his years. David's life on earth was riddled with consequences for his sins. Absalom, his son, tried to overthrow and kill him only to be killed by David's men. David was constantly at war and shedding blood. One of his sons from his multiple wives (also sin) raped his half-sister, and David failed to enact justice. God did not allow David to build His Temple. And so on. There is wonderful, powerful assurance that God will forgive the debt of our sins if we are in Christ. But we can never lose sight of the fact that our sin has consequences on this earth.

Sin always matters. Just ask the repentant sinner whose sin has put them in jail for life, or worse, on death row. Or just ask the children of divorce. Even when mom and or dad are forgiven, their children will always be impacted. Ask the people whose anger, lust, or dishonesty has destroyed relationships. God always offers forgiveness, and often there is reconciliation. But for so many, the consequences last for years.

The consequence of our sin is another reason we can't take sin lightly. We should all be so thankful for the redemption given through Jesus Christ and celebrate the fact that the sin from which we have been forgiven will never be held against us by our Holy Father. But God's grace can never be an excuse to take sin lightly. God will surely forgive the repentant leader, but many will never be in leadership again. So, we must be cautious not to play the David Card when we sin. David's earthly life was never the same. His sin was removed. The consequences were not.

DAY 13

Sin Distorts Conviction

> *[3] But Peter said, "Ananias, why has Satan filled your heart to lie to the Holy Spirit and to keep back for yourself part of the proceeds of the land? [4] While it remained unsold, did it not remain your own? And after it was sold, was it not at your disposal? Why is it that you have contrived this deed in your heart? You have not lied to man but to God." [5] When Ananias heard these words, he fell down and breathed his last. And great fear came upon all who heard of it.* - Acts 5:3–5

Are you familiar with the moment in Church history described in Acts 5:3-5? It's a big moment when God clarifies that He takes sin seriously. If you go back and read the entire account documented by Luke in Acts chapter 5, you will find that at the end of Acts 4, Barnabas sold some land and gave all the money to the church. Ananias decided to bring some money in from some property that he had sold and pretended to give all of it to the church. Sadly, he decided to bring his wife in on this little scam.

What was the problem? Ananias and his wife wanted to get the accolades for sacrificially giving without actually sacrificing. They decided to pocket a little for themselves. Let's be clear: they were not obligated to sell their land or to give any of the proceeds, much less all, to the church. But they were obligated to be honest and not pretend to give it all to the church. This sin revealed much about these two.

When Peter calls out Ananias (and later his wife Sapphira), he says something significant: "Why has Satan filled your heart to lie to the Holy Spirit"? Peter is pointing out that this wasn't a mistake. This wasn't a stumble. This was something Ananias planned out, and what Peter wants to know is, "Where is the conviction"? Peter was curious: if Ananias truly had the Holy Spirit and was part of the Church, how did he lie and scheme so easily? Ananias' sin was so powerful in his life that he didn't feel the conviction of the Holy Spirit. Or maybe there was no conviction because Ananias and his wife were both fakes.

Peter points out that Ananias doesn't even realize the gravity of the situation. How could Ananias not realize he wasn't just lying to Peter and the members of the congregation but that He was lying to God? Maybe the bigger question is, do you and I see our sin this way? When we so carelessly sin like Ananias, we forget that we are not just sinning against people, but that we are sinning against God. God clarifies just how seriously He takes this rebellion. He killed Ananias on the spot. I love that Luke then lets us know that great fear came across everyone who heard it. I bet it did! Has a great fear come across you after you were reminded of Ananias' fate today?

Sin will always distort our convictions. We must examine ourselves and ask ourselves about any "pretending" we have going on. Pretending to be devoted to Jesus, i.e., saying the right things or standing up for the right causes, but knowing deep down this is just lip service, will only fool those around us. God knows our hearts, and He requires true love and devotion. Remember, any "acting" in our lives isn't just a lie to people; it is a lie to God.

DAY 14
Sin Limits Our Ability to Serve

Not many of you should become teachers, my brothers, for you know that we who teach will be judged with greater strictness. - James 3:1

James wasn't happy with what he saw in the congregation as he led the first church in Jerusalem. Where we pick up in James 3, he has just written his well-known passage on faith without works. James wasn't saying that works earn salvation for us, far from it. He was saying that a saving faith comes with fruit as evidence of redemption. Our righteous works are proof of our salvation.

James illustrated this point by looking at the example of Abraham. Abraham wasn't considered righteous by God because he "believed" God wanted him to sacrifice his son Isaac. No, he was deemed righteous when he packed up everything needed for the fire, took the knife, made his way up the mountain, put his son on the altar, and raised that same knife to slay Isaac. Abraham's actions proved he had a faith so strong that he completely trusted that whatever God said to do was justified. God, of course, did not require Abraham to sacrifice his son, but Abraham was so certain of God's promises through Isaac that he trusted that God had a plan. Abraham proved he had an unwavering faith in God.

James begins chapter 3 by addressing those who sit in a position of authority as teachers. Some of these teachers did not show a resolve like Abraham's when it came to living out their faith. And James said this failure may disqualify them as teachers. Why? Because James says teachers are held to the highest standards regarding their integrity. James says that when God gives anyone the responsibility of teaching His Holy Word, that person must live a life that doesn't send a message of inconsistency. In the rest of chapter 3, he goes on to say that the sin that troubled him the most is that, apparently, these teachers could not control their tongues.

James addresses how we sin with what we say. He wrote that many teachers, and Christians in general, bless God with the same tongue they use to curse people. James correctly points out that this sends a terrible message to those they teach. James 3:13 says that by good conduct, we show those we teach that we have wisdom. Think about that for a moment. James is saying if you can't control your behavior, you lack the wisdom required to be a teacher.

Take a step back and think about exactly what James is saying. He's saying that our sin can and does limit our ability to serve God. What a shame it is to be called to a specific role and to answer the Spirit's leading, only to find ourselves disqualified from serving because of our sin. Sin matters.

Are you serving the church? I hope you are. There are few greater joys in life. But if you are, let me encourage you, in love, to look at your life and your attitude toward sin. Are you fighting it? Or are you just giving in? Should you be in leadership? Do you have the type of control over the sin in your life that you can be trusted by God to teach and lead?

DAY 15
Sin Affects Those Around Us

> *And to Adam he said, "Because you have listened to the voice of your wife and have eaten of the tree of which I commanded you, 'You shall not eat of it,' cursed is the ground because of you; in pain you shall eat of it all the days of your life."* - Genesis 3:17

As we're about halfway through this in-depth look at sin and grace, it's fitting that we should revisit the place where it all went down. We're picking up in Genesis in the aftermath of Adam and Eve's rebellion against God and God's subsequent judgment against them. In Genesis 3:17, we see God addressing Adam, beginning to pronounce His judgment on Adam's sin. But something interesting happens before we get to this point.

When God learns of their sin, He looks for Adam and Eve. But see how Scripture describes this: "[8] And they heard the sound of the LORD God walking in the garden in the cool of the day, and the man and his wife hid themselves from the presence of the LORD God among the trees of the garden. [9] But the LORD God called to the man and said to him, "Where are you?" (Gen. 3:8–9). Have you ever noticed that when God showed up in the garden after Adam and Eve committed the very first sin, He wasn't looking for Eve? I mean, you would think God would want to speak to the one who gave into Satan's tempting and failed the test that resulted in the downfall of the earth and all of humankind! And yet, Genesis 3:9 tells us that God was looking for Adam, asking him, "Where are you?" Why is this significant?

God didn't call Eve, and God didn't ask Adam for the location of his wife. No, God wanted to talk to Adam, the one to whom He had entrusted the information about what was forbidden and what wasn't. In Genesis 2:16–17, it says, "[16] And the LORD God commanded the man, saying, 'You may surely eat of every tree of the garden, [17] but of the tree of the knowledge of good and evil you shall not eat, for in the day that you eat of it you shall surely die.'" God addressed Adam first because Adam was responsible for both him and Eve keeping God's commandments. But apparently, Adam had decided to either neglect the duty of correctly passing on to his wife exactly what God said, or he did not communicate the seriousness of it. Eve was then deceived because Satan was able to say, "Is that what God really said?" (3:4-6). Then, not only did Eve eat the fruit, but Adam did as well. And thus, humankind has dealt with their rebellion ever since.

Adam wasn't tempted by Satan, but he was held accountable for his apathy because he did not properly lead Eve but instead chose to be apathetic, and now all humankind must pay the price. Adam's sin didn't just affect him. It affected Eve, their children, and the entire human race. And Eve's sin didn't only affect her. Adam was cursed right alongside her. Her decision, and Adam's decision to follow her lead, had devastating implications. Their story highlights an important truth: rarely does our sin only affect us. Sin almost always affects those around us.

What sin are you allowing in your life and your home? It won't just hurt you. Is today the day you take seriously the damage that your unchecked sin is having on you and those you have been called to lead? Sin matters to God. Does it matter to you?

DAY 16
Sin Takes Away Our Peace

> *[20] "But the wicked are like the tossing sea; for it cannot be quiet, and its waters toss up mire and dirt. [21] There is no peace," says my God, "for the wicked."* - Isaiah 57:20–21

I can still remember when I lived as a wicked man. The words of Isaiah 57:20–21 were so evident in my life. I was speaking about my past with a small group of young men one night, and I told them that my life had not gotten easier since I had decided to repent and follow Jesus. I told them there was no guarantee that life would ever cease to be a challenge, but I could promise them one thing: no matter how much pain my devotion to Christ had brought me, the peace that resulted from my redemption far exceeded it.

Do you have peace? When I was a defiant sinner, the consequences for my sin seemed to be around every corner. Who had I lied to? Would I go to jail? Who was I in conflict with, and when will I be found out? And so on. There was no peace in my life. And just like God said through Isaiah, the loudness of my sin disturbed my sleep. I was tossing and turning, unable to find contentment and always looking for the next pleasure that surely would bring contentment. And yet, all I would do was churn up more mire and dirt.

What changed all that? What appeased God's anger? Look at Isaiah 57:15-16: "[15] For thus says the One who is high and lifted up, who inhabits eternity, whose name is Holy: "I dwell in the high and holy place, and also with him who is of a contrite and lowly spirit, to revive the spirit of the lowly, and to revive the heart of the contrite. [16] For I will not contend forever, nor will I always be angry; for the spirit would grow faint before me, and the breath of life that I made." What appeased God's anger was when I finally had a contrite heart and a lowly spirit. I stopped justifying my sin and cried out to God to hear, forgive, and change me. You see, the wicked that God speaks about in verses 20 and 21 are those who do not have a contrite heart and who do not have a lowly spirit. Or, to put it another way, those who still think much of themselves and very little of God. It takes humility to admit that we are sinners.

Sin matters to God. God will always oppose the proud person who is dead in their sins. But grace matters to God, too, and He will always lift the lowly in spirit who come to Him in repentance. God is looking for a heart willing to soften and cry out for God to give it new life. Are you ready to acknowledge that sin makes God angry, and God's anger can only be appeased by our humble faith in Christ that leads to sincere repentance? If we want peace, we must believe and repent, and then as God promises, our restlessness will be replaced with a perfect, lasting peace.

DAY 17
Sin Keeps Us In Spiritual Infancy

> *[1] So put away all malice and all deceit and hypocrisy and envy and all slander. [2] Like newborn infants, long for the pure spiritual milk, that by it you may grow up into salvation—[3] if indeed you have tasted that the Lord is good.* - 1 Peter 2:1–3

1 Peter is a letter from Peter to the church during a time of tremendous persecution. Where we pick up in 1 Peter 2, Peter just finished calling on church members to be holy. Peter is telling the church to never compromise the standard! Jesus is the standard for those saved by faith in Him, and the power of the Spirit – the same power that raised Christ – should flow from all who are redeemed. In chapter 2, Peter turns to the action that needs to be taken in order to continue to grow spiritually and be ready to do the work of the Lord.

What is step 1 in Peter's plan to see Christians grow in maturity? Remove sin! Why? Because it stands in the way of spiritual growth. Peter makes a challenging point. He asks whether we desire to grow up spiritually. I can honestly say that at one point in my spiritual life, I was only concerned about my redemption and did not have much desire to grow up spiritually. How about you?

Peter continues this line of thinking by telling us we should be like newborn infants and long for spiritual milk so that we may grow up spiritually. Peter uses the analogy of a newborn baby because the redeemed have been born again. A baby comes into the world needing his mother's milk to grow and thrive. But maybe your wife has had the challenging experience of having a baby that did not show much interest in nursing. It's so common that labor and delivery nurses have a pretty standard plan for addressing this. If a baby comes into the world without much longing for the nutrients its mother provides, doctors and nurses will try to get the baby to taste the milk in order to understand that it is good. Often, all it takes is for the baby to taste the milk to awaken the natural longing for it. The baby can't help but want the sustenance God intended for it to have in order to grow.

Peter teaches us that the first thing we must do to awaken our longing for this spiritual milk is to remove the sin in our lives. We must put sin away. We must clear our lives of the sin-habits that numb our desire for the Lord.

Notice the word "if" in verse 3. Please don't overlook it. "If indeed you have tasted that the Lord is good." Peter leaves that option open. Maybe the reason malice, deceit, hypocrisy, envy, and slander are still prominent in our lives is that we have a longing for sin that exceeds our longing for the Lord. We haven't tasted, i.e., experienced, that God is uniquely and perfectly good.

Are we willing to take action today? Are we willing to take the steps to grow up and leave spiritual infancy? One thing will always stand between us and true intimacy with God: unrepentant sin. Are we willing to put away all that holds us in spiritual infancy and keeps us from thriving?

DAY 18
Sin Destroys Relationships

[25] Therefore, having put away falsehood, let each one of you speak the truth with his neighbor, for we are members one of another. [26] Be angry and do not sin; do not let the sun go down on your anger, [27] and give no opportunity to the devil. - Ephesians 4:25–27

Steve Farrar is one of the many mentors God brought into my life that contributed to my sanctification. Steve has received his eternal reward from the Savior he served so well, but I still often recall his wisdom. I recall him teaching us that Jesus took on human flesh and lived out a perfect example of how to do everything correctly, including being angry. Did Jesus get angry? Yes, but Jesus' anger was righteous. He was angry without sinning. Can you and I say the same thing about our anger?

Paul is writing to the Ephesians about the new life Jesus provides those who come to saving faith in Him. Paul spends a lot of time discussing practical things that everyone who claims to be justified by grace through faith in Christ should implement in their lives. In verse 4:25, Paul says we should all be honest with each other. Don't lie to your neighbor or be disingenuous in any way because we are one body now. Then, he hits the topic of anger in verse 26. Here, Paul gives us a warning about the wrong kind of anger.

Paul says that it's possible to be angry and not sin. His first advice is to not let the sun go down on our anger. Don't let it fester! Boy, I have ignored this advice far too many times. Have you ever been angry with someone, and as the hours go by, what they did or said becomes more and more horrible? "How dare they say that! Have they forgotten how hard I work? To think of all I've done for them, and this is how they treat me?" Paul advises us to go to the person, tell them why we are angry, and work it out before something worse happens.

Did you know that the devil loves when we rant and rave because he knows the longer we let anger burn, the more likely we are to sin? If the devil can get us to go from angry to livid, he knows the more likely it is that he can shred relationships. I know families and friends who got upset about something, and they not only let the sun go down but have let years go by, ruining the relationship. Satan loves this result.

Look at Ephesians 4:32: "Be kind to one another, tenderhearted, forgiving one another, as God in Christ forgave you." Wow! How dare I deny forgiveness to others when God did not deny it to me? God did not let the sun go down on our sins without offering us a chance to repent and be forgiven. Why don't you pick up the phone today and tell that person why you are angry and start the reconciliation process? You will likely discover some sort of misunderstanding, maybe something you didn't have right, or something that would have been resolved long ago if you had simply followed God's instruction and not let the sun go down on your anger.

There is such a thing as righteous anger. We have to be careful that our anger doesn't lead to destroyed relationships. God cares too much about you and whomever it is that has angered you to watch your emotions destroy opportunities to glorify Him.

DAY 19
Unchecked Sin Diminishes Credibility

[1] "Judge not, that you be not judged. [2] For with the judgment you pronounce you will be judged, and with the measure you use it will be measured to you. [3] Why do you see the speck that is in your brother's eye, but do not notice the log that is in your own eye? [4] Or how can you say to your brother, 'Let me take the speck out of your eye,' when there is the log in your own eye? [5] You hypocrite, first take the log out of your own eye, and then you will see clearly to take the speck out of your brother's eye. - Matthew 7:1–5

We have an entire generation of people inside and outside the church who think the only thing Jesus ever said was Mathew 7:1: "Judge not, that you be not judged." If you listen to the masses, this is the sum of Jesus' teaching. Interestingly, Jesus not only said more than these words, but most people also don't correctly apply the concepts Jesus teaches here.

Jesus isn't saying in Matthew 7 that no one can say that another person's behavior is immoral or sinful. If this were the case, then the entire ministries of every Old Testament prophet and much of the New Testament epistles would be negated. Paul tells Timothy that Scripture is powerful in part because it is useful for rebuking and correcting others (2 Tim. 3:16). Also, Paul makes it clear in 1 Corinthians 5:12-13 that we are called to address sinful behavior within the church, but we must do so correctly. Jesus isn't saying we can never call sin what it is. What Jesus is saying is that we cannot be hypocrites.

Jesus is on record for caring as much about the attitude in which we do things as He is about the things we do. Jesus reminds us that we must understand that the same measure of right and wrong, His measure, applies to us and not just to the person we stand ready to correct. Jesus says the one thing that makes us unable to remove a speck from another person's eye is to have a log in our eye. If we can't hold ourselves to God's standards, we have no credibility to hold anyone else accountable.

To help our brothers and sisters with the sins in their lives, we must first check the sins in our own lives. Does this mean we must be perfect before working to help others? No. We will always struggle with our sinful nature on this side of heaven. But Jesus reminds us that to correctly point out any deliberate and perpetual inconsistency in our brothers' lives, we better make sure we don't have them in our lives. We will live the Christian life with specs in our eyes; it's our spiritual inheritance from Adam and Eve. But we must be careful we don't walk around with eyes full of the logs of our sin-habits.

So, I guess this is bad news for those who would like to think that Jesus would never ask them to be held accountable to their brothers and sisters in Christ. Jesus desires for us to hold each other accountable and walk with each other together toward righteousness. (He even clarifies that if we are willing to remove the log in our eye, we can see clearly to remove the speck from our brother's eye.) But being a hypocrite will absolutely destroy your credibility. If we decide to address sin in someone else, let's make sure we have stopped tolerating the sin in our lives. If we haven't, then we risk losing our creditability. And once credibility is lost, it can be a long road to gaining it back.

DAY 20
Sin Decreases Intimacy with God

> *[3] There is no soundness in my flesh because of your indignation; there is no health in my bones because of my sin. [4] For my iniquities have gone over my head; like a heavy burden, they are too heavy for me. [5] My wounds stink and fester because of my foolishness, [6] I am utterly bowed down and prostrate; all the day I go about mourning.* - Psalm 38:3–6

The wonderful preacher and pastor Adrian Rogers once said, "I would not present the best 15 minutes of my life before a holy God." Wow. Isaiah 64:6 further clarifies that our most righteous deeds are nothing but filthy rags in the presence of our God. Dr. Rogers and Isaiah were both right. In Psalm 38, David begins to process this same truth. Here, we get a picture of David understanding that his sin is an abomination to God. His sin has become more than he can handle. Here, we see him mourning that his sin has caused him to lose intimacy with God.

Look at verse 3. David clearly says he cannot find peace because he knows that his sin has brought God to anger. What does it mean that God is "indignant"? To be indignant isn't a mild response. To be indignant is to be affronted and insulted. Sin is an insult to God. If only we truly understood this.

David was not brought to repentance when the prophet Nathan pointed out how David had treated Uriah. David changed his tune when Nathan pointed out that David had sinned against God. You and I can always find some selfish way to falsely justify our mistreatment of other fallen people, but brothers, we can never find justification for sinning against God. After all, this is the one who graciously forgives our iniquities by sacrificing Himself to redeem us from a standard we could never achieve. Perfect, holy Jesus became sin on our behalf so that we might become holy (2 Cor. 5:21). How can our response to this truth cause us to still be so flippant about sinning against Him?

In today's passage, David confesses that he is burdened because of sin against God. He considered himself dirty. This awareness finally moves him to true repentance, and he acknowledges that he is in this position because of his foolishness. Ultimately, we only have ourselves to blame when we continue in sin after knowing the standards of God.

What David sensed is that sin destroys intimacy with God. David's sin had created a distance between God and him. Do we realize that God's holiness makes it impossible for Him to be near sinful humanity? When we continue to justify perpetual deliberate sin in our lives, we put a relational barrier between God and us. In love, God will turn us over to the repercussions of our sin in order to allow us to feel what David felt so that we might repent and turn back to Him. For many, the thing that turns them back to God is feeling the separation and distance that unrepentant sin causes.

Look back at verse 6. Here, David begins to mourn his sin. Brothers, we must mourn the sin in our life because then we take on God's view of sin, not our own. This is critical. We must stop looking at sin through our fallen, delusional eyes and see sin the way God sees it. He hates it, and we must hate it as well.

DAY 21
Sin Defiles the Church

> *[1] It is actually reported that there is sexual immorality among you, and of a kind that is not tolerated even among pagans, for a man has his father's wife. [2] And you are arrogant! Ought you not rather to mourn? Let him who has done this be removed from among you.* - 1 Corinthians 5:1–2

Church discipline is not enjoyable, and anyone looking forward to carrying it out is a bit off. But let me tell you something worse than enjoying church discipline: refusing to deal with it. Too often, people are too quick to lean on "grace" and "who are we to judge" as excuses to let unrepentant sin go on. But here in 1 Corinthians 5:1-2, we see that Paul is quite upset with the fact that sexual immorality is being allowed to go unchecked in the church body. Why is Paul so angry? Because Paul knows that sin defiles the church.

What we will discuss today is very important and often grossly misunderstood. Paul is distinguishing between how we treat the lost in the church versus those who claim to have already been redeemed. In verse 2, Paul uses the phrase "removed from among you." Now look at 1 Corinthians 5:11-13. Here, Paul says that he warned the Corinthians to not even associate with anyone who claims to be a brother (or sister) who continues to live a life of open, deliberate, unrepentant sin and continues to justify it as if it were OK. Paul isn't saying not to associate with church members who make mistakes. If that were the case, none of us would be able to hang out with each other.

Paul makes it clear that there is a different call on how we respond to the lost outside of the church versus those who claim to be part of the church. Look at verses 12 and 13 in 1 Corinthians 5. Paul clarifies that God judges those outside the church, but the church should hold its members accountable for their unrepentant sins. We miss this so badly on both ends of the spectrum.

Why does Paul say this church member living in open sin should be removed? First, because it might save the man's life. Yes, Paul says in verses 3-5 that they should turn the offender over to Satan for destruction because if he suffers the consequences of his sin, he just might repent and be saved on the Day of the Lord. What a concept! Too many times, we keep bailing people out, or people keep bailing us out when we are rebelling against the very God who saved us. Furthermore, open, deliberate sin, like what was being practiced in the Corinthian church, defiles God's Bride. Paul knows that sometimes people need to suffer the consequences of their sins before they will repent.

Next, Paul says you must remove this person because the church must stay pure. If you let this kind of sin go by thinking you are being so gracious, others will be impacted, and soon, the church will be deeply impacted by it. Unchecked sin always produces more sin.

We need to get this right. We spend too much time concerned about who can be let in the church building and very little time, if any time, concerned about who should be removed. Who can come in? Anyone who professes faith in Christ. God judges the lost; we don't. But who should be escorted out? Anyone who claims to be redeemed but refuses to repent of open, perpetual, deliberate sin.

Church discipline is extremely difficult, but it's necessary for the sake of the individual and the Body.

PART 3

Our Attitude Toward Sin

DAY 22
The Severity of Unchecked Sin Will Increase

> *[6] The LORD said to Cain, "Why are you angry, and why has your face fallen? [7] If you do well, will you not be accepted? And if you do not do well, sin is crouching at the door. Its desire is contrary to you, but you must rule over it."* - Genesis 4:6–7

Cain and Able is a well-known story, but today, let's look at the role sin plays in this historic event and learn from the lesson. After sin entered the world, it didn't take long for the first murder to take place. It appears jealousy is as old as time. Recall that Cain killed his brother Able because God approved of Able's offering and not Cain's. The text doesn't tell us exactly why God honored Able's offering and not Cain's, but we can read between the lines and form a pretty good idea of what's happening.

Cain had no one to blame but himself. He brought an offering that was unacceptable to God. He brought fruit from the ground while Able sacrificed a firstborn lamb from his flock. So, at the outset, there's the idea that Able's offering was more sacrificial, more valuable. And yes, there is a connection to the Levitical law that would come later. But Bible scholars make a great point: one sacrifice isn't automatically better than the other; it's the spirit in which they are given. God, who knows the thoughts and motives of each of us, recognized Able's sacrifice as more honorable, likely because it was more sacrificial, but also because of Able's heart when he made it.

When God didn't honor Cain's offering as He did Able's, it angered Cain. This is the first mistake. Cain didn't show any remorse or concern that he had displeased God; instead, he found God unreasonable, taking no responsibility for his sin. Cain wasn't just mad at God for correctly rejecting his offering; he doubled down and hated Able for doing the right thing because it won God's approval.

Cain wasn't furious with himself for his sin; he was furious with Able for his righteousness. If only Cain's sin would have stopped there. But unfortunately, that's not the way sin works.

God still tried to help Cain with a warning. God knew Cain was about to make a huge mistake if he didn't check himself. God warned that sin was crouching at the door, and Cain must rule over this sin. Cain refused to deal with his sin against God and jealousy of his brother. The refusal to heed God's warning led to the escalation from jealousy to the first taking of innocent life. Cain went from the sin of anger and jealousy to being a murderer.

When unchecked sin is allowed to flourish, the severity of our sin often increases. It may not lead to murder, but an unchecked "emotional" affair often leads to a physical affair. An unchecked sin of covetousness or greed has led some to steal from their company. An unchecked eye that looks at unwholesome images can lead to a porn addiction. You "slip up" and get "tipsy" a few times, and the next thing you know, you're regularly getting drunk. Maybe an unchecked sin of apathy toward worship leads to leaving the church altogether.

Each of us has a sin-nature. We will never be able to live a sin-free life, which is why it's fitting to stop and praise God for His gift of grace and restoration through faith in His Son, Jesus. We will always contend with sin. But hopefully, this devotional has helped remind us that there is no such thing as a "little" sin-habit. Sin always matters, in part because sin snowballs. Little sin-habits give birth to big sin-habits. And big sin-habits can destroy us. Just like Cain. What sin-habit in your life is crouching at your door that you must work with the Spirit to finally overcome?

DAY 23
Sin Reveals a Lack of Wisdom

[15] Look carefully then how you walk, not as unwise but as wise, [16] making the best use of the time, because the days are evil. [17] Therefore do not be foolish, but understand what the will of the Lord is. [18] And do not get drunk with wine, for that is debauchery, but be filled with the Spirit. - Ephesians 5:15–18

In these verses, Paul is waving a caution flag. "Look carefully then how you walk." Do you and I look carefully at how we walk, i.e., live out our Christian faith? If not, we're ignoring Paul's warning, and to do so reveals a serious lack of wisdom. We would do well to focus on his words today.

Paul urges the Ephesians (and us) to watch how we walk, live in wisdom, and see our time as incredibly valuable. Paul says that "the days are evil," and if you and I are not careful how we spend our time, we will be caught up in sin.

How do you spend your time? Men ask me quite often what they should do to grow up spiritually. We are men, so we want to know the game plan. My response is always simple: take the same passion, energy, time, and devotion that you apply to everything else you love and deem of value and apply it to your faith. I have noticed that when I spend my time wisely and focus on things that matter to God, I usually don't struggle with sin. Unfortunately, I have found the opposite to be just as true; when I spend my time unwisely focusing on things of this world, I struggle with my sinful nature. How we view our time matters.

Paul says the one thing we must do to wisely live the Christian life is to understand the will of the Lord. This is a big deal because Jesus tells us in Matthew 7:21-23 that only those who do the will of God are His true disciples. How do we know the will of God? Read the Bible. Scripture paints a perfect picture of what God wants from His children.

So the question is, do you know the will of God? Are you wise in the scriptures? Do you know when you are doing something that is not the will of God? One thing that is the will of God is found in I Thessalonians 4:3, where Paul writes, "For this is the will of God, your sanctification." How are you doing on that one? Are you growing up spiritually?

If we return our attention to our passage for today, we see Paul offering us an example of the kind of behavior that is an obstacle to our pursuit of wisdom: drunkenness. Many of you want to turn the page as you read this but stay with me. I have a simple question for anyone reading this who struggles with moderating their alcohol use. Be honest with yourself: Is it wise to be intoxicated or unwise? If you're honest, you must admit that when a person is intoxicated, they are prone to do, say, and think things they would never do while sober. Not to mention what we know to be true about alcohol's impact on our health. This is why Paul uses this example.

The sin of drunkenness is a sin that is not only unwise but also leads us down a path that only increases in foolishness. Paul says those who abuse alcohol find themselves participating in all sorts of debauchery. Paul says the wise stay away from the sin of drunkenness and instead fill themselves with the Holy Spirit, which gives them discernment to be in God's will, not against God's will. Drunkenness is not the only sin that leads us down this road. So many sin-habits lead us away from wisdom and not toward it. If you have a sin-habit that has dominated your life, it's time to carefully look where you walk and choose wisdom over foolishness. What grace God has awaiting you! What redemption He offers when we repent and return to Him. He is faithful and true. When we turn away from sin, He will always be there waiting to restore us.

DAY 24
Sin Reveals a Lack of Faith

[26] For if we go on sinning deliberately after receiving the knowledge of the truth, there no longer remains a sacrifice for sins, [27] but a fearful expectation of judgment, and a fury of fire that will consume the adversaries. - Hebrews 10:26–27

Look at Hebrews 10:26–27. Here, the author of Hebrews clarifies that the only possible way for us to be redeemed of our sins is through the sacrifice provided by Jesus Christ. In verses 19-25, the author urges his audience to hold fast to the truth that our hope of redemption is found in Jesus, the perfectly faithful one. Jesus was faithful to God's eternal plan to fully pay the sacrifice due for the penalty of humankind's sin. Only Jesus makes it possible for those who repent and place their faith in Him to have peace with God today and eternal life in the future. He is the propitiation for our sins, taking God's wrath on Himself to provide redemption. In verse 24, the author of Hebrews writes that the power of this redemption then begins to produce good works in us.

However, in verse 26, the author shifts his tone. He says that the opposite is also true. Suppose our response to the knowledge of all that God has done for us through the sacrifice of His Son, Jesus, is to continue to deliberately sin. In that case, we should not expect forgiveness but judgment. Notice the word "deliberate." The author makes the Holy Spirit-inspired point that he isn't talking about a stumble or a mistake. The process of sanctification is just that: a process. We battle our sin-nature every day, and this will continue to some degree until our glorification. But these are stumbles followed by conviction from the Holy Spirit and continued repentance and correction. This isn't what the author of Hebrews is saying.

In these verses, we see the description of a person who knows the truth about redemption, refuses to repent, and continues to deliberately sin. There is no sense of contending with sin or attempting to resist temptation. This can only mean that they were never truly redeemed in the first place. Their deliberate, intentional sin tells the truth about their spiritual condition. After all, if we are truly saved by faith in Christ, we can never lose our salvation because of our sinfulness. If we could, our faith would be works-based, which isn't how salvation works. So what the author of Hebrews is saying here is that the person who has heard and understood the Gospel but remains committed to sin could not possibly be saved. Instead of God's grace, mercy, and approval, we experience through saving faith in Christ, they will experience God's righteous wrath.

Revelation 20:11-15 provides us with a chilling vision of what will happen to those who died without ever coming to saving faith in Christ. John pictures the dead standing before the great white throne of God. There are books that contain the sins of every person who has ever lived. But there is another book: the Book of Life. For those whose names were not in the Book of Life, their sins condemn them to eternal separation from God. Only those whose names were in the Book of Life, those who had been saved by God's grace through faith in Jesus, survived to spend eternity with God in the new heaven and earth.

Maybe you've grown up in church your whole life. Maybe your parents were solid Christian people. Maybe you're a "good person" who lives a "good life." Apart from being born again by saving faith in the person and work of Jesus Christ, none of that will earn you salvation. Only saving faith in Jesus will. Hearing and understanding the Gospel won't affect your standing before God. Only believing in the Gospel will. And when we are truly redeemed, our attitude toward sin will never be the same.

Are you a Christian in name only? Or, because of your faith in Jesus, is your name written in the Father's Book of Life? How you answer this is the most important thing you will ever do.

DAY 25
Jesus Died for Our Sins, Not Our Excuses

> *[13] No temptation has overtaken you that is not common to man. God is faithful, and he will not let you be tempted beyond your ability, but with the temptation he will also provide the way of escape, that you may be able to endure it. [14] Therefore, my beloved, flee from idolatry.* - 1 Corinthians 10:13–14

I was raised by a man who absolutely hated excuses. If you wanted my father to launch, refuse to take responsibility for a mistake. When my dad was coaching, if I or any player failed to do their job, made an excuse, or refused to take responsibility for our lack of excellence, my dad would always say, "Just tell me that you didn't get the job done and don't make an excuse; own it and correct the mistake."

Today, we will look at one of the New Testament's most abused and incorrectly used verses. Sadly, many have incorrectly taken these verses and decided they mean that God will never give you more than you can handle. Am I the only one who has already been through many trials and tribulations I could not handle on my own? If God will ensure that life will never throw anything at us that we can't handle, then why do we need Him? This thinking has always been absurd and does not survive biblical scrutiny. God allows many struggles and trials to come into our lives to break us of our self-reliance so that we might depend on His strength because we cannot handle the burden on our own. For some bonus reading today, read 2 Corinthians 12:1-10 and you will see this point being made quite clearly.

The key to understanding exactly what these verses mean is to read all of 1 Corinthians 10. When you do, you see that Paul is talking about sin, not calamity. Paul is warning the church that they should not make the same mistake the Israelites made when they sinfully chased after idols, sexual immorality, gluttony, drunkenness, and other wicked pursuits. Paul reminds the Corinthians that because they now have the Holy Spirit, there is no excuse to give into the temptation to sin. Why? Because there is no temptation so strong that God couldn't deliver them from their sinful desires. The same is true for us today.

Paul goes on to say that God will always give you a way out, an exit. What we must learn to do is to take the way out that God always provides. Paul says that if we give into sin, it isn't because God isn't strong enough to enable us to endure the temptation. It can only be that in that moment, we wanted to sin. There is no excuse!

Can any of us honestly say that when we sin, it was because we were tricked into it or just couldn't help ourselves? No, I can honestly say that any sin that still trips me is due to me simply not being mature enough spiritually to access the power of God to overcome the desire. How bout you? Are you still, making excuses for the sin that is still in your life? Stop. Just say you didn't get the job done. Own the mistake. Repent and commit to lean on God. Grow up spiritually so the Holy Spirit will lead you to the way out that God always (not sometimes) gives us.

DAY 26
Secret Sin Is Rebellion Against God

> *And he deposed the priests whom the kings of Judah had ordained to make offerings in the high places at the cities of Judah and around Jerusalem; those also who burned incense to Baal, to the sun and the moon and the constellations and all the host of the heavens.* - 2 Kings 23:5

Josiah became king of Judah when he was eight years old. In 2 Kings 23:25, we see that "there was no king like him, who turned to the LORD with all his heart and with all his soul and with all his might, according to all the Law of Moses, nor did any like him arise after him." So, what made Josiah so unique?

What made Josiah unique was how he stacked up to the kings that came before him. Except for a small minority, most kings before Josiah were wicked. Some of the more godly ones instituted reforms, most notably Hezekiah, but none were as sweeping as Josiah's. He did something that none of the kings were willing or able to do: he didn't just remove some of the false idols that had captured the people's hearts; he removed them all.

The other kings of Judah who tried to make reforms and turn the people back to God failed to address the worship of pagan gods in the high places. Why? It's hard to say for sure, but it might have been that they were hedging their bets. They were mostly faithful to God but not completely. Many of them had secret sins.

We know well what secret sin is. Stuff like fudging your tax returns. Or being jealous of what someone else has. Maybe it's secretly lusting for another woman or looking at pornography in secret. Maybe it's drinking alcohol in secret. A secret sin is any sin that is easy to hide, and we continue to embrace because we want redemption from God without repenting or turning away from all sin. We prefer to only repent of some sins, many of which we don't struggle with anyway.

Many of the other kings before Josiah would do away with the idols that were easy to remove, but they would not put in the effort to go up into the high places and destroy the altars to pagan gods. I have talked openly about my struggle with gluttony. A friend who is training me asked me after I had gone down a few sizes in clothing if I had thrown away or donated my former larger clothes. When I told him I had not, he warned me that I was hedging my bets. He said hanging on to my old clothes was me saying that I was not truly done with being overweight. He said that when I am resolved that this is my new life, I will not use those larger clothes as a safety net in case I put the weight back on.

Josiah's reforms were intentional and aggressive. He removed anything and everything that was blaspheming God. Not some things; all things. He restored the worship of God and the observance of the Law and justified nothing that opposed God. Have you? Have I?

We must ask a tough question today: have we destroyed all the idols in our lives or just some of them? Have we turned away from sin that was never a struggle but secretly held on to some sin that pleases us? If so, we still love our sins more than we love submitting to God. Sin matters to God, always. We must fight all sin, especially the sin we think we're hiding. Because, in truth, there is no hiding anything from God.

DAY 27
Approving Sin is Rejecting God

Though they know God's righteous decree that those who practice such things deserve to die, they not only do them but give approval to those who practice them. - Romans 1:32

Read Romans 1:32. The Apostle Paul wrote the book of Romans while he was in Corinth, one of the most sinful and debased cities of that day. Isn't it possible that Paul is looking at the state of this sinful city while he writes these strong words to the Romans?

The first phrase of verse 32 is very intriguing: "Though they knew God's decree." This tells us that Paul is speaking about people who are not ignorant of the decrees of God. These are people, like I was at one time in my life, who were very aware of what sin was. But, like I used to, they not only practiced the very things God said not to do but approved others who did the same things. Now, the part here that jumps out at me is that Paul says not only do these people know God's standard, but they also seem to be fully aware that the result of these sins is death. It's a stark contrast between what they knew and what they did.

To fully grasp what is happening here, we also need to look at Romans 1. Paul says in Romans 1:28, "And since they did not see fit to acknowledge God, God gave them up to a debased mind to do what ought not to be done." These people are aware of God and might even believe in God, but they have decided not to acknowledge God's standard. Sadly, I can relate to this inconsistency.

I have never been agnostic or an atheist. I have no period of my life that I did not believe in God. But I do recall denying God's standard for a very long period of my life. Instead of repenting, leaving my authority, and submitting to God, I lived under my standards, fully expecting God to redeem me anyway. God was ready to transform me into something He could approve of, but I decided to become God's PR agent and attempt to make Him into something I could approve of. God does not need humans to make Him more palatable. I did not realize that by trying to make God into something easier for me to deal with that I was actually rejecting Him altogether.

Here is something to consider: Could it also be possible that we continue to ignore God's standard because, though we claim to believe in Him, we just don't? Is it possible to believe that because we are participating in and approving of sin, we have not yet been transformed by saving faith in Jesus? Have you ever thought of it that way? Paul says if we continue on a road of unrepentant sin that God would give us up to a debased mind so that we will learn the hard way that He is right and we are wrong. His standard is for our good. The most life-giving thing a person can do is to accept God and His standards and live in the freedom that comes from submission.

DAY 28
Love of Sin Sends a Costly Message

> *[15] As morning dawned, the angels urged Lot, saying, "Up! Take your wife and your two daughters who are here, lest you be swept away in the punishment of the city." [16] But he lingered. So the men seized him and his wife and his two daughters by the hand, the LORD being merciful to him, and they brought him out and set him outside the city.* - Genesis 19:15–16

Today, we look at the tragic decision to teach our families or those whom we influence to love sin. Read Genesis 19:15-16. Recall how we got to this historical event. First of all, Lot decided to settle his family in Sodom. He grossly miscalculated the influence sin would have not just on him but on his wife, daughters, and future husbands. Lot had been discipled by his uncle Abraham and, by all accounts, was a man of God. But he decided, like many of us, to be what I call a "sin daredevil." And it almost cost him everything.

A sin daredevil is someone who goes toe-to-toe with sin. Instead of avoiding it, they surround themselves with it but try to stay untouched by it. These people foolishly and arrogantly believe they can be around sin and it not affect them. Lot was such a man.

Don't miss that when we get to Genesis 19, Abraham has already had to go and rescue Lot from being taken captive by kings who had defeated the king of Sodom. Lot returned to this city of sin. Why? Because he loved Sodom and all that came with that city of sin. The problem with living a life as a sin daredevil is that it sends a message to anyone in their lives that they love sin more than they love God. When they suddenly wake up and warn others, they have no credibility.

If you read verse 14, you will notice that God sent angels to get Lot and his family out of Sodom before their sins brought God's righteous judgment. But Lot's sons-in-law laugh at him. He tried to warn them, but they thought he was joking. Why? Because all they ever saw was a man who loved Sodom. He hesitated even when the angels told him to get his wife and daughters and flee. Lot isn't quite sure he wants to give up his sin.

Does Lot ever get right with God? Apparently, so. Peter refers to him as righteous in 2 Peter 2:6-9. But what about his wife, sons-in-law, and daughters? In Genesis 19:26, we see his wife so yearned for Sodom she had to look back to mourn its destruction. As a result, God turned her into a pillar of salt. Who taught her to love Sodom so much? Her husband, Lot.

Love of sin sends a costly message. What sins are you and I teaching our wives and children to love? This is very serious. If you and I do not take our sanctification seriously and continue to flirt with sin to the point we bring that garbage into our lives and homes, we may cause those who trust us to get the wrong message about repentance and sin. And that confusing message could cost them their eternal lives.

DAY 29
Tolerating Sin Shows a Lack of Zeal

> *[6] And behold, one of the people of Israel came and brought a Midianite woman to his family, in the sight of Moses and in the sight of the whole congregation of the people of Israel, while they were weeping in the entrance of the tent of meeting. [7] When Phinehas, the son of Eleazar, son of Aaron the priest, saw it, he rose and left the congregation and took a spear in his hand [8] and went after the man of Israel into the chamber and pierced both of them, the man of Israel and the woman through her belly. Thus, the plague on the people of Israel was stopped.* - Numbers 25:6–8

Have you ever heard anyone say that one of the heroes of the Bible is Phinehas? Well, God considered him so devoted that his zeal for Him moved God to turn back His wrath from the people of Israel. This is one of the wilder stories in Scripture. If it's new to you, buckle up.

Why was God's wrath being poured out on His people in the first place? Take a guess. If you guessed sin, you would be correct. God told His people time and time again that they should not worship foreign gods and they should not marry women who worshipped foreign gods. But that didn't stop many of the Israelite men from being intimate with the daughters of Moab. As God knew they would, these women began to lead these men to the worship of their pagan gods.

God ordered Moses to kill all the leaders who were participating in this sin in order to turn away His anger. While grieving over this terrible state of affairs and the judgment their sin had caused, one of the Israelite men paraded into the camp, in front of Moses and the entire congregation, with a pagan woman. He took her and went right into his family's tent to be intimate with her. Phinehas was Aaron's grandson, and when he saw this, he took a spear, went into the tent, and drove it through both their bodies while they were in the act of sin.

What was God's reaction to this sudden and violent act? Approval. Why? Because God recognized Phinehas' zealousness for God. In the midst of a people who could be brazenly defiant to the God who had led them out of slavery, finally, here was someone who took God's law so seriously that he would go to the greatest lengths to protect God's glory. In turn, God says that this zeal for God's glory and hatred of sin caused God to remove His wrath from His people and not consume them with His righteous jealousy (vs. 10-11).

Now, one thing can't be missed: not only did the man and woman that Phinehas speared lose their life, but verse 9 tells us that 24,000 other people were killed by the plague that God handed down before His wrath was turned back. Brothers, sin always matters. There is never a moment when sin doesn't matter to God.

What turned back God's wrath? Someone willing to stand up for His glory. Someone to finally say, "Enough"! Someone to say, "I will not stand here and let the God who redeemed me be blasphemed any longer." Now, this doesn't mean we are called to spear anyone! We would be wrong to sin in our zeal. But we are called to stand for God's standard and begin to see sin as He does.

God considers sin to be an affront to His glory. Do we? Are we willing to be men so jealous for God's glory that we would stand up for Him against a world that hates Him? It's those kinds of men that God is looking for.

DAY 30
Sin Must Be Confronted

[29] If your right eye causes you to sin, tear it out and throw it away. For it is better that you lose one of your members than that your whole body be thrown into hell. [30] And if your right hand causes you to sin, cut it off and throw it away. For it is better that you lose one of your members than that your whole body go into hell. - Matthew 5:29–30

If you or your family were being attacked by anything that might lead to their death, would you just casually take it on? Of course not! If you took an apathetic approach to a life and death situation, it could easily cost you or a loved one their life. Why, then, do we so often let sin hang around our lives as if sin poses no real threat to us or the people we claim to love? If this resource accomplishes nothing else, I pray that God will use it to wake us up to how seriously He takes sin. I pray we will wake from our slumber to realize that sin is a big deal and should never be taken lightly.

In today's passage from Matthew 5, Jesus is speaking about the severity of sin and how the sin in our lives must be dealt with aggressively. When it comes to our sin, passivity is very dangerous. Jesus says whatever is in our lives that is causing us to sin, we must remove it aggressively. He uses the phrases "tear it out" and "cut it off." Are you ready to look at your life and be bold enough to honestly assess what needs to be torn out or cut off? Are we ready to treat sin as if it were poison that, if consumed, would kill us or someone we love?

Jesus says it's better to be one-eyed and one-armed and go to heaven than to have two eyes and two arms while spending eternity in hell. Brother, is that "friendship" with the female that isn't your wife worth it? Are the images you look at on your phone really worth your eternity? Is the job that causes you to sin worth the money you make from doing it? Is the alcohol that you can't quite get under control and keeps causing you to sin worth all the regret?

Jesus tells us to tear it out and cut it off if it causes us to sin. This includes idols that we have built in our lives. Is that hobby worth you not being immersed in the church on Sundays? Do your obsessions cause you to neglect being the spiritual leader of your home? Do you lack biblical understanding because you make time for everything but time in the Word of God? Jesus reminds us again that we may see sin as no big deal, but that doesn't mean He does.

God is so serious about our sin that He would rather us tear out a sinful eye and cut off a sinful arm than continue in the sin. That is an extreme reaction that shows exactly where He stands. What things or people might need to be torn out of or cut off from your life to be made right with God?

DAY 31

I Am the Problem

But each person is tempted when he is lured and enticed by his own desire. - James 1:14

I have a dear friend who passed away in the last couple of years who, for many years of his life, was a raging drug addict. This addiction led to so many other sins and run-ins with law enforcement. His name is Bill Searcy, and I can't wait to see him again in eternity. Bill finally repented of his sin, left faith in himself, and declared Jesus Christ the Lord of his life. Jesus radically changed this man and used him to bring many others to Christ.

Bill often told the story of his ever-changing communities and journeys in and out of various rehab facilities. Many times, when he would be sitting in front of the latest counselor, he would be told that to stay clean, he needed to find a new place to start over so he could get away from all the people who were horrible influences on him. After hearing this same line of thinking from yet another counselor, Bill looked at the counselor and said, "I hear you, but the problem is everywhere I go, there I am." My dear friend knew that in that season of his life, he was his own worst enemy.

James, the half-brother of Jesus, didn't believe in Jesus until his brother died on the cross, was resurrected from the grave, and came back to say hello. James went from calling himself the brother of Jesus to calling himself a servant of Jesus. James was a hard-nosed, straightforward man. If you read about the Jerusalem council in the book of Acts chapter 15, you will see when the Jews and Gentiles argued over some issues concerning the church. They finally send for James, and Luke says no one opposed him.

In James 1:14, James is telling this new church in Jerusalem the same thing that my friend Bill had come to understand. James said that he still saw too much sin in the congregation. He heard that some were saying that God was tempting them. James says clearly that the person to blame for their sin is themselves. James and Bill would have probably gotten along.

Brothers, can I point out the obvious? Unlike God, Satan isn't omnipresent, omniscient, or omnipotent. He can't be everywhere. Is it true that Satan tempted Jesus? Yes. Is it true that Satan has targeted some of the saints of God himself? Yes, again. But is it likely that Satan himself would abandon whatever he is doing to personally go after you and me? I would think that isn't likely. So what is the issue? James is telling us that our sin-nature is what is causing us to sin. We are lured and enticed by our own desire.

When we are redeemed by saving faith in Jesus, our dead spirit becomes alive for the first time. We are given the Holy Spirit as a guarantee that one day, we will be with God forever. Our fleshly, sinful nature is in tension with the Spirit within us. The battle rages. But here's a truth: When we feed the Spirit, we starve the flesh.

We must stop playing games with our flesh by placing ourselves in bad situations. We must stop being sin daredevils! Let's stop searching Scripture for what God allows while skipping what He commands. Let's stop seeing how close to the line with alcohol we can get. Let's stop flirting with that woman who isn't your wife. James warns that attitude will conceive and give birth to sin, and when it's fully grown, it will bring forth death. When that happens, it won't be the devil's fault. It will be ours. Apart from Christ, we are the problem.

CLOSING

Thank you for taking this 31-day journey and not being afraid to ponder the overwhelming grace of God in the face of sin. As you wrap up your time in this book, I want to encourage you to be cautious not to elevate God's love, mercy, and grace above His judgment. We must realize that truth and love are equal pillars; one isn't more important than the other. Of course, we shouldn't speak only of God's wrath and judgment, but we must also be leery of only speaking of God's grace and mercy.

If we refuse to talk about the seriousness of sin, then people may get the notion that they don't need a savior. Why do I need a savior if there really isn't anything I need to be saved from? Think about the woman at the well. Jesus started out talking to her about her need for living water. He told her that the living water He offered would satisfy her so that she would never thirst again. When she expressed a desire for this living water, Jesus turned to why she needed Him. What was the reason? Her sin. Jesus told her to go get her husband, and she answered that she had no husband. Jesus then told her that He knew that was true, and not only that, but that she had been married five times and wasn't married to the guy she was currently living with.

How did the woman respond to Jesus? She recognized that there was something different about Jesus. She recognized that Jesus was a "prophet," in her words. Of course, Jesus goes on to tell her that He was the Messiah, God's Son, sent to take away the sins of the world. After hearing this, the woman ran to the city to tell everyone who Jesus was. Don't miss this: her testimony to the validity of Jesus' claim to be Messiah was that He told her all she had ever done. Faced with her sin, she recognized her need for Jesus. Her brokenness led her to a new life in Christ.

If we are never willing to discuss the severity of sin, people may never see themselves for who they are and may never reach out for a Savior who can rescue them from death and eternal separation from God. The repulsiveness of my sin makes me so grateful for God's redemption.

Jesus said it best when He told the woman who was about to be stoned by self-righteous men. Jesus pointed out that only He could condemn people because He was the only one with no sin. And yet, He chose not to condemn her, demonstrating His grace and mercy. But in the face of His compassionate response to her, how did He end the conversation? He said something that is all too often left out: "Now go and sin no more." Why did Jesus end the interaction like this? Because sin always matters.

ABOUT THE AUTHOR

Rick Burgess has been the cohost of the *Rick and Bubba Show* since 1994, a nationally syndicated radio show which airs to 1.2 million people weekly. Rick has coauthored multiple New York Times bestselling books, the *How To Be A Man* series of 40-day devotionals, *Transformed*, and numerous articles. As a commentator and guest, Rick has appeared on various radio and television shows, including *Fox and Friends* and the *Sean Hannity Show*.

Rick is a frequent speaker at church services and marriage conferences, but his true passion is men's ministry. As Founder of *The Man Church*, Rick calls on the modern church to put into practice what they say every Father's Day, that a man's family will follow him if he leads them.

He has been married to the former Sherri Bodine since 1996. Rick's Spirit-filled message at his youngest son's memorial service was the most-watched YouTube video in the world the week it was posted.

IRON HILL

press

---

on Hill Press is a collective of people who love Jesus, love Gos-
el truth, and love sharing those things with others through the
medium of publishing and gospel-centered event experiences.
Learn more about us at ironhillpress.com.

ironhillpress.com   888.969.6360